VOLCANO!

The 1980 Mount St. Helens Eruption

by Gail Blasser Riley

Consultant: Daniel H. Franck, Ph.D.

BEARPORT
PUBLISHING COMPANY, INC.

New York, New York

Credits

Front cover (main), Austin Post, USGS/Cascades Volcano Observatory; Front cover (inset), Craig Mitchelldyer/Getty Images; Back cover (top), Donald A. Swanson, USGS/Cascades Volcano Observatory; Back cover (bottom), Peter W. Lipman, USGS/Cascades Volcano Observatory; Title page, Craig Mitchelldyer/Getty Images; 4–5, John Barr/Liaison/Getty Images; 6, Vince Streano/CORBIS; 7, David Muench/CORBIS; 8–9, © Gary Rosenquist 1980; 11, Mauro Fermariello/Photo Researchers, Inc.; 12, Dave Herring; 13, Kevin Schafer/Peter Arnold, Inc.; 14, Dave Herring; 15, Joe Carini/Pacific Stock; 16, Dan Dzurisin, USGS/Cascades Volcano Observatory; 17, Lyn Topinka, USGS/Cascades Volcano Observatory; 18, Roger Werth/The Daily News, Longview, Washington; 19, Roger Ressmeyer/CORBIS; 20, Jim Nieland, U.S. Forest Service, Mount St. Helens National Volcanic Monument, CVO/USGS; 21, Lyn Topinka, USGS/Cascades Volcano Observatory; 22, Roger Werth/The Daily News, Longview, Washington; 23, Macduff Everton/CORBIS; 24, USGS/Cascades Volcano Observatory; 25, AP/Wide World Photos; 26, Lyn Topinka, USGS/Cascades Volcano Observatory; 27, Dave Harlow, USGS/Cascades Volcano Observatory; 28, AP/Wide World Photos.

Original design and production by Dawn Beard Creative, Triesta Hall of Blu-Design, and Octavo Design and Production, Inc.

Library of Congress Cataloging-in-Publication Data

Riley, Gail Blasser.
 Volcano! : the 1980 Mount St. Helens eruption / by Gail Blasser Riley.
    p. cm. — (X-treme disasters that changed America)
 Includes bibliographical references and index.
 ISBN 1-59716-072-5 (lib. bdg.) — ISBN 1-59716-109-8 (pbk.)
 1. Saint Helens, Mount (Wash.)—Eruption, 1980—Juvenile literature. 2. Volcanoes—Washington (State)—Juvenile literature. I. Title. II. Series.

 QE523.S23R55 2006
 551.2109797'84—dc22

                              2005028041

For more information, write to Bearport Publishing Company, Inc., 101 Fifth Avenue, Suite 6R, New York, New York 10003. Printed in the United States of America.

1 2 3 4 5 6 7 8 9 10

Table of Contents

Escaping Disaster

A huge cloud of steam, gas, and rocks **exploded** from the volcano. "Let's get out of here!" Joel Harvey yelled. His ten-year-old son, Jo-Jo, dashed with his family and friends into the car. Was there still enough time to outrun the fiery **ash** and flying rocks?

Jo-Jo sobbed as the car slid back and forth across the road. Rocks rained down on the roof. Lightning flashed as hot mud flowed down Mount St. Helens.

The car's headlights shone into total darkness. Clouds of black ash had blocked the sunlight. "Daddy, are we going to die?" Jo-Jo asked.

◀ Mount St. Helens erupted in Washington State at 8:32 A.M. on May 18, 1980.

Rocks, gas, and ash from an exploding volcano can travel 10 to 11 miles (16 to 18 km) in just one minute!

A Sleeping Giant Awakes

Mount St. Helens had not **erupted** since 1857. On March 20, 1980, however, an earthquake shook the ground below the mountain. A small amount of steam and ash rose from the volcano. Scientists **predicted** it would soon erupt. The sleepy volcano's 123-year nap was about to end.

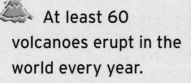 At least 60 volcanoes erupt in the world every year.

This scientist watches small ▶ amounts of ash come out of Mount St. Helens a month before the volcano's eruption.

Jo-Jo and his family had come to Mount St. Helens with Gary Rosenquist. Gary had wanted to get very close to the volcano so that he could take pictures of it as it began to erupt. The group camped about 10 miles (16 km) from the mountain. Taking pictures of the eruption would be a historic event.

▲ People often camped in the beauty around Mount St. Helens. After the 1980 eruption, campers weren't allowed to return for seven years.

Earthquake! Avalanche!

On the morning of May 18, when Gary was taking pictures of Mount St. Helens, an earthquake rocked the ground. Within seconds, the whole north side of the mountain collapsed. Ice, snow, rock, soil, and trees roared toward the foot of the volcano at 155 miles per hour (249 kph). It was the biggest known **avalanche** in recorded history.

▲ This photo, taken by Gary, shows the volcano beginning to erupt at 8:32 in the morning.

The avalanche triggered a volcanic explosion. Steam, gas, and thousands of pieces of rock blasted out of the mountain. They sped through the sky at over 600 miles per hour (966 kph). Smoke and ash shot 12 miles (19 km) high.

Volcanic ash contains tiny, sharp rock **particles.** If the ash gets sucked into planes flying nearby, it can cause the engines to stop working and make the planes crash.

▲ Mount St. Helens exploding

Dozens of Eruptions

The 1980 eruption was not the first time Mount St. Helens had blown its top. The volcano is thousands of years old. Up until 1857, it had erupted more than 30 times. Then the volcano became **dormant**. The eruptions stopped for over 100 years.

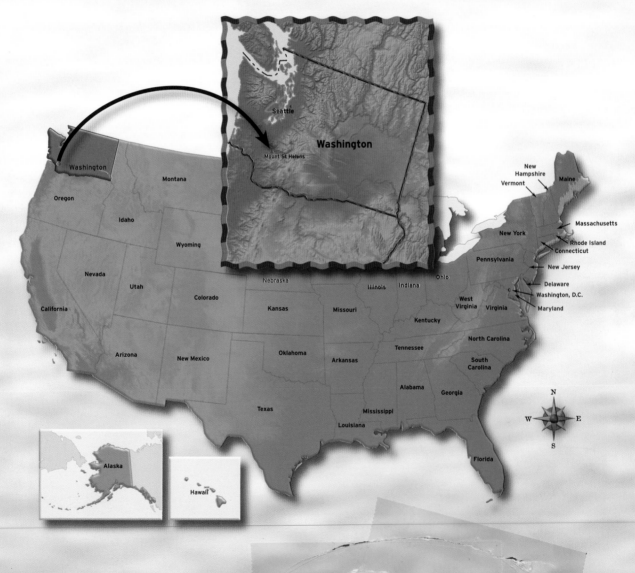

Many scientists predicted Mount St. Helens would erupt again before the year 2000. They thought they knew the future for the volcano. As Jo-Jo and his family found out, they were right!

▲ Scientists use this thermometer to measure the ground temperature around volcanoes. It helps them predict when a volcano might erupt.

Volcanologists are scientists who study volcanoes. They sometimes must run from eruptions when they are working near dangerous volcanoes.

What Is a Volcano?

Earth's surface is a rocky **crust**. Below the crust is rock that is so hot it can stretch and flow. This hot rock is called **magma**. When magma comes all the way up to Earth's surface, it is called **lava**. A volcano is the place where lava shoots out of Earth's crust.

Volcano Erupting

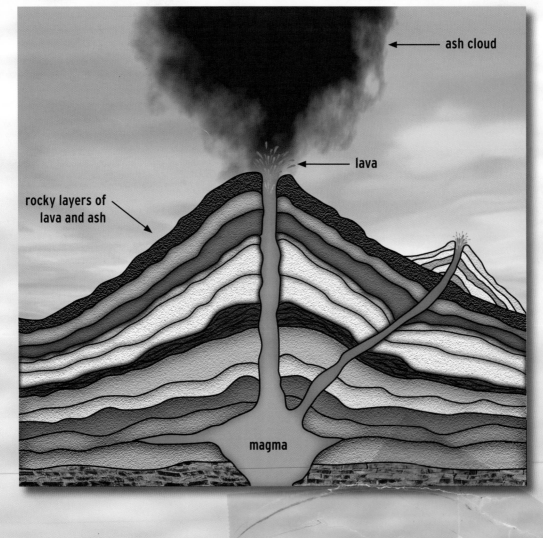

ash cloud

lava

rocky layers of lava and ash

magma

When blazing hot lava cools, it turns into rock. Each time a volcano erupts, layers of lava and ash may build up on the sides of the volcano. After many eruptions, the rocky layers can form a tall volcanic mountain.

▲ Volcano in Costa Rica

Some of the biggest volcanoes began forming on the ocean floor. Over millions of years, the lava built up around the volcanoes until they reached above the water's surface to form islands.

Where Are Volcanoes?

Volcanoes form around the world. Earth's crust is made up of large slabs of rock, called plates. These plates are like broken parts of a giant eggshell. Most of the world's **active** volcanoes are found on the edges of Earth's plates.

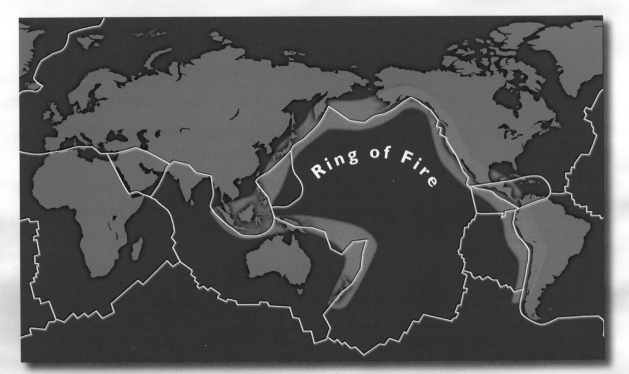

Ring of Fire

▲ The white lines show the edges of Earth's major plates.

About 90 percent of the world's active volcanoes are located along the edge of the Pacific plate in an area called the "Ring of Fire."

The plates move slowly on top of magma. Where plates press against one another, there are earthquakes. Sometimes, one plate moves down under another one. Many cracks then form in the plates. The lower plate may heat up and become magma. Over time, the magma can bubble up through Earth's surface to form a volcano.

▲ Lava shooting up through cracks in Earth's plates

Escape Between Blasts

The first blast from Mount St. Helens lasted for about 15 minutes. It seemed the mountain might be going back to sleep. Jo-Jo and his family were able to drive out of the darkness to safety. Others, however, were not so lucky.

▲ A newspaper photographer was trapped and found dead in his car ten miles (16 km) from the volcano.

Some volcanic eruptions last for just a few hours while others continue for over a year.

The volcano erupted again. It continued for nine hours. Over 200 square miles (518 sq km) of forest were flattened. Burning ash and rock from the mountain started fires. Blasting wind snapped some trees like toothpicks. It yanked others out of the ground. Even the soil was blown away.

▲ The Mount St. Helens blast destroyed more than 10 million trees.

Mudflow

The heat from the blast melted ice and snow high up on the mountain. The water rushed down mixing with ash and pieces of rock. Soon everything flowed to the ground as a dangerous **mudflow** at speeds of up to 80 miles per hour (129 kph).

▲ Homes were swept away by the mudflow.

Meanwhile, the avalanche **debris** swept thousands of trees into Spirit Lake. They raised the water level 100 feet (30 m). Hot mud and rock also poured into the lake. All life in the water was killed. The temperature shot up from a cool 42°F (6°C) to nearly 100°F (38°C).

▲ Trees still covered a large part of Spirit Lake in 1992.

The blast from Mount St. Helens was so strong that it ripped trees from hillsides as far away as six miles (ten km).

Blowing Its Top

Mount St. Helens actually blew part of its top off when it erupted. After the blast, the volcano was about 1,313 feet (400 m) shorter. A piece of the mountain as tall as the Empire State Building had been blown away. In its place was a new one-mile-wide (1.6-km) crater in the shape of a horseshoe.

▲ **Before the eruption**

After the blast, plants and trees no longer dotted the volcano's north side. Instead, ash and dead plants fanned out in a gray mess. Some animals had raced away to safety. Yet about 5,000 deer, 1,550 elk, and 200 black bears were killed.

▲ After the eruption

Volcanoes can build back the parts they lose if lava continues to flow out of them and cool into hard, rocky layers. Scientists say Mount St. Helens could build back its lost part in about 100 years.

Refusing to Leave

During the deadly eruption, 57 people lost their lives. One 84-year-old man, Harry Truman, refused to leave his home at the foot of the mountain. Harry was with his 16 cats when rocks from the blast crashed down at over 100 miles per hour (161 kph). No one ever found him or his cats.

▲ Harry Truman at home with his cats before the eruption

Some people on the mountain died because of the great heat from the eruption. Others died as they tried to escape. Their **lungs** filled up with ash and gas. They could not get any air to breathe.

▲ The blast from Mount St. Helens crushed this car.

The Mount St. Helens explosion destroyed 250 homes and smashed seven bridges. It ruined almost 200 miles (322 km) of roads.

Life Comes Back

Volcanoes destroy crops and forests when they erupt. Yet they also give life back. They spit out lava and ash. When these materials mix with bits of dead plants on the ground, they make new soil. Plants can then begin to grow again.

Scientists studied the changes that were happening on the mountain. They learned how dead and fallen trees play an important role in helping new life begin. They used this information to teach others not to remove woody debris when trees are cut down. In 1994, a government plan to protect forests was created based on what scientists learned from Mount St. Helens.

◀ An elk near Mount St. Helens in 2004

Plant roots can survive a volcanic explosion. As they grow, they push their way back up from far underground. Over time, new stems and leaves will grow from the roots.

Warnings for the Future

Mount St. Helens taught scientists that a volcano can erupt with little warning. So after the explosion, scientists worked to find new ways to detect early signs of volcanic activity.

Scientists made movable machines that check for changes of gases in the air, and temperatures in the ground. The machines also check for a slight shaking of the land.

▲ Scientists measure cracks at Mount St. Helens. If the cracks get wider, it means the volcano might be getting ready to erupt.

Mount St. Helens is an active volcano. It could erupt again at any time, so scientists watch it closely.

This new information helps scientists better predict when a volcano might erupt. Earlier warnings mean people will have more time to prepare before an eruption so that more lives can be saved.

▲ The lessons scientists learned from studying Mount St. Helens helped them accurately predict the 1991 eruption of Mount Pinatubo in the Philippines.

Just the Facts

About Mount St. Helens

- The greatest dangers from the Mount St. Helens eruption did not come from lava, but from ash, steam, and **poisonous** gases.

- Helicopter pilots rescued more than 100 people trapped on the mountain after the 1980 eruption.

- Mount St. Helens erupted six more times in 1980. Each eruption was much smaller than the one in May.

- In 1982, the government set aside 110,000 acres (44,515 hectares) around Mount St. Helens as a national monument.

- Native American names for Mount St. Helens include Loo-wit (Keeper of the Fire) and Tah-one-lat-clah (Fire Mountain).

Mount St. Helens released ▶ steam and ash again on October 5, 2004.

About Volcanoes and Eruptions

- Seventy-five percent of the biggest eruptions during the past 200 years have come from volcanoes that had never erupted in recorded history.

- There are about 1,900 active volcanoes in the world.

- Almost nothing stops volcanologists from their work. Seven volcanologists went to study the Galeras volcano in Colombia, South America. It erupted as they were working. Six of the researchers lost their lives because they were crushed by huge rocks or burned. Volcanologist Stanley Williams was lucky. His skull and legs were broken, but he lived. When he got well, he went back to studying and visiting volcanoes again.

Glossary

active (AK-tiv)   a volcano that releases gas and lava, even in small amounts

ash (ASH)   tiny volcanic pieces of rock and minerals that are less than .08 inches (2 mm)

avalanche (AV-uh-lanch)   large amounts of snow, ice, or rock sliding down a mountain

crust (KRUHST)   the top or outside layer of something

debris (duh-BREE)   pieces of something that has been destroyed

dormant (DOR-muhnt)   a volcano that has not erupted for a very long time, but could erupt again

erupted (i-RUPT-id)   sent out lava, ash, steam, and gas from a volcano

exploded (ek-SPLOH-did)   burst

lava (LAH-vuh)   hot rock that comes out of cracks in Earth's surface; the rock is so hot that it can bend, stretch, and flow

lungs (LUHNGZ)   parts of the body in a person's chest that are used for breathing

magma (MAG-muh)   blazing hot rock inside Earth that can bend, stretch, and flow

mudflow (MUD-floh)   mud that moves quickly down the outside of a volcano or mountain

particles (PAR-tuh-kuhls)   very small pieces

poisonous (POI-zuhn-us)   something that is deadly

predicted (pri-DIKT-uhd)   told what would probably happen in the future

Bibliography

Carson, Rob. *Mount St. Helens: The Eruption and Recovery of a Volcano.* Seattle, WA: Sasquatch Books (2000).

Scarth, Alwyn. *Vulcan's Fury: Man Against the Volcano.* New Haven, CT: Yale University Press (2001).

- volcano.und.nodak.edu/vwdocs/msh/msh.html
- www.fs.fed.us/gpnf/mshnvm/

Read More

Adams, Simon. *The Best Book of Volcanoes.* New York: Kingfisher (2001).

Lauber, Patricia. *Volcano: The Eruption and Healing of Mount St. Helens.* New York: Aladdin Paperbacks (1986).

Magloff, Lisa. *Volcano.* New York: DK Publishing (2003).

Learn More Online

Visit these Web sites to learn more about volcanoes:

- www.nationalgeographic.com/volcanoes/
- www.pbs.org/wnet/savageearth/volcanoes
- www.volcano.si.edu/world/

Index

About the Author

Gail Blasser Riley is the author of more than 35 books for children and adults. Her books have received honors from the Children's Book Council, New York Public Library, and Young Adult Library Services Association.